D1195878

"Fountain Cemetery"

Fostoria, Hancock Co., Ohio

1911 – $2,000 – granite

Civil War Monuments of Ohio

by Harold A. George

"Ohio's Veterans Home"
Sandusky, Erie Co., Ohio
September 17, 1988 - bronze

"Woodside Cemetery"

Middletown, Butler Co., Ohio

December 17, 1902 – bronze/stone

Civil War Monuments of Ohio published by Harold A. George

Additional copies of this book may be ordered directly from the author by mail at 14513 Bayes Ave., Lakewood, Ohio 44107, or via email at **ninthohio@core.com**.

The information contained in this book is accurate to the best of the author's knowledge. The author and publisher assume no liability whatsoever for errors or omissions of any kind. This book may depict areas that are privately owned; such depiction does not mean these areas are open to the public. Always obtain permission from the owner before entering or crossing any private property.

Created, produced, designed and published in the United States of America by H.George Publishing.

Printed in Mansfield, Ohio, by *Book Masters Inc.*

First edition, May 2006

ISBN Number: 0-9728183-1-6

Library of Congress Control Number: 2006900513

"Glendale Cemetery"
Cardington, Morrow Co., Ohio
July 4, 1889 – white bronze

Monument's original location:

Center of Cardington, at the intersection of East Main and Center Street. The monument was moved to Glendale Cemetery in August 1889.

Table of Contents

Table of Contents

"Cemetery"
Ohio City, Van Wert Co.., Ohio
May 30, 1903 – bronze

"*Spring Garden Cemetery*"
Cincinnati, Hamilton Co., Ohio
1866 - $25,000 - bronze/granite

Acknowledgement

More than six-years of field work, thousands of miles driving throughout the state, and countless hours spent in libraries and historical societies have gone into this project. However, it could not have been completed without the aid of others.

I wish to extend a thank you to the following individuals and institutions who provided me with their assistance, support and expertise: Ms. Anne Kling, Archives Manager, Cincinnati Historical Society Library; Mr. Joseph Lackman, local historian, Apple Creek, Ohio; Library Staff, Bristolville Public Library; Cemetery Sexton, Washington C.H., Ohio; Staff, Butler County Soldiers & Sailors Monument, Hamilton, Ohio; Mr. Randy Bergdorf, Director, Cuyahoga Valley Historical Museum, Peninsula, Ohio, and Cemetery Sexton, Glendale Cemetery, Akron, Ohio.

I wish to further thank Mr. James Hudkins of Cuyahoga Falls, Ohio, for his suggestions, encouragement and support with this project.

"Christmas on the Square - Soldier at Parade Rest"
Bedford, Cuyahoga Co., Ohio
July 3, 1886 - $2,000 - granite

"Greenlawn Cemetery"

Columbus, Franklin Co., Ohio

Introduction

Between the years 1861 and 1865, nearly four-million Americans participated in the American Civil War (2.5- 2.75 million for the North and 750,000 - 1.25 million for the South). Ohio contributed 311,000 volunteers to the cause .... 35,475 did not survive the war. Ohio's contribution included enough volunteers to support the formation of 198 Infantry Regiments, 27 Cavalry Units, and 28 Artillery Batteries (2 heavy and 26 light). Even before the war was over, the decision was made to create monuments to recognize the sacrifice contributed by Ohio's sons. In 1863, the state's first monument was erected and dedicated in the small village of Bristolville, Ohio. The monument honored Bristolville's fourteen sons who had volunteered to serve the cause and had paid the ultimate price.

At the same time, Cincinnati collected funds for a similar monument to be built. The monument, a statue of a soldier with his rifle and bayonet, was completed and dedicated in Spring Grove Cemetery in 1865. Before the decade was over, eight additional towns erected monuments for their towns. To date, there are well over 250 monuments in the Buckeye State.

Of the 88 counties in Ohio, only three counties (Clinton, Noble and Pike) do not have a statue or other instruments to recognize their civil war veterans. Five counties have more than ten monuments each:

Hamilton (17)   Lucas (15)   Lorain (13)   Brown (12)   Franklin (10)

1996 - 9th Ohio Civil War Re-enactment
Mesopotamia, Trumbull Co., Ohio

(L. to R.) Ron Luikart § Mark Carmin (deceased)
John Barnett § Patrick Lawlor

Town Square
Warren, Trumbull Co., Ohio

Ohio's First Civil War Monument

In June 1861, two young men from Bristol (Bristolville), Trumbull County, Ohio, boarded a wagon bound for Warren, Ohio, with their ultimate destination being the American Civil War. Every few months thereafter this same routine was repeated until August 1862, when a total of 14 sons from Bristol were serving their country.

Starting in April 1862, mothers in Bristol began receiving word, either by telegraph, letter, or the newspaper accounts of battles, that their son had been killed in the war. The same bad news continued to be received until only one of the original fourteen remained alive. Then, on August 13, 1863, Charles A. Brooks, Adjutant with the 7th Ohio Volunteer Infantry, was killed in a freak railway accident in Cleveland, Ohio. Now there was no longer any sons from Bristol serving their country. . . They were all dead.

At the urging of Myron D. Phelps, Bristol's most public spirited citizen, $500 was collected to design a memorial to honor those fourteen brave souls. On October 16, 1863, a dedication ceremony was held in Bristol's town square.

A procession of thirty-four young ladies, dressed in white, with pink scarves, representing the thirty-four states in the union, paraded thru the square. They were precede by the Marshall and a brass band. When they arrived at the site, two young ladies removed the flag that covered the monument and the brass band struck up, "Rally Round the Flag".

At the same time, a tableau was exhibited, representing the Goddess of Liberty. Fourteen small boys with heads bowed, standing beside stacked arms, represented the fourteen soldiers.

Sculptured near the top of the marble monument is the inscription, **"Defenders of the Union"**. At the base of the monument is carved, **"Erected and Dedicated to the Memory of Our Honored Dead from Bristol, Ohio"**. On the side of the monument is carved the names of the fourteen dead sons, ages 17 - 44.

A Sad Accident at the Depot

At about nine o'clock last evening, an omnibus, occupied by five persons, was crossing the track near the depot, when it was struck by some Toledo cars. One of the passengers leaped out and succeeded in avoiding the car and another, **Charles E. Brooks**, Adjutant of the 7th Ohio Volunteer Infantry, made the attempt, when he was struck down and the car passed over both his legs, cutting the left one completely off below the knee and crushing the right ankle and foot. He was taken to the New England House and surgical aid was called in, but nothing could be done to save him. He died early this morning.

Adjutant Brooks has served in the 7th with great credit and bravery, and had been detailed from the regiment to bring on the drafted men. His mother lives in Trumbull county.

Cleveland Plain Dealer
**Thursday
August 14, 1863**

"Ohio's First Civil War Monument"
Bristol(ville), Trumbull Co., Ohio
October 15, 1863 - $500 - marble

Monument Changes Over the Year

For the most part, the Ohio civil war monuments have not changed since they were first erected. However, there are many instances where the surrounding features have changed.

On the following pages you will see a picture postcard, showing the way the monument looked when it was dedicated, together with a recent photograph showing the current condition of the monument and surrounding area.

Cincinnati, O. Avondale Public School and Lincoln Monument.

Avondale Public School
Cincinnati, Hamilton Co., Ohio
Dedicated December 2, 1902 – bronze/granite

1910 postcard

2006 photograph

Note: The school shown in the postcard, behind the monument, is now gone.

Soldiers & Sailors Monument, Cleveland, Ohio.

Sept. 19. 1905
Mrs B.

1905 postcard

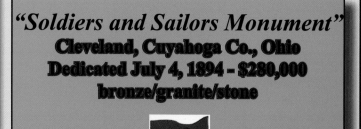

"Soldiers and Sailors Monument"
**Cleveland, Cuyahoga Co., Ohio
Dedicated July 4, 1894 – $280,000
bronze/granite/stone**

2004 photograph

1900 postcard

"Riverview Cemetery"
East Liverpool, Columbiana Co., Ohio
Dedicated May 31, 1889

2004 photograph

Note: The rotunda on the top of the monument is now missing.

1909 postcard

"Birchard Public Library"

Fremont, Sandusky Co., Ohio
Dedicated August 1, 1885 - $7,600 - granite

2006 photograph

Note: The library is still there, more than 100 years later.

Monument and Entrance to High and Main Street Bridge,
Hamilton, Ohio

Nov. 24. 1910.
a.o.t.

1910 postcar

"Butler County Soldiers, Sailors & Pioneers Monument"

Hamilton, Hamilton Co., Ohio
Dedicated July 4, 1906 - $3,250 - bronze/stone

2004 photograph

Note: The iron bridge in the postcard, after 100+ years, was torn down for a new bridge the week before this photograph was taken.

Steedman Monument, Toledo, Ohio.

1911 postcard

"General Steedman Monument"
Toledo, Lucas Co., Ohio
Dedicated 1887 - $25,000 - bronze/marble

2006 photograph

Note: The iron fence, lamp posts and pillars are now missing.

Monument Builders

In the 1800's, there were two primary companies that built the monuments and memorials in Ohio.

Monumental Bronze Company of Bridgeport, Connecticut

The Monumental Bronze Company was organized and established in Bridgeport, Connecticut in 1874. It proved to be a very successful enterprise.

White Bronze was in use at the end of the 19th century, primarily for statuary and garden furniture. It was touted as being more durable and permanent than stone, but never really caught on with the general public as a material for grave markers. The Monumental Bronze Company (with six foundries, including one in New Orleans), was the only firm that made white bronze grave markers. With the lack of interest in white zinc as a material for monuments, even the Monumental Bronze Company ceased manufacturing them shortly after the turn of the century.

Unlike their stone counterpart, these monuments resisted weathering and most survive in excellent condition. Metal tombstones and monuments are over a century old and are rust-free. These monuments were cast in pure zinc. Zinc forms a coating of zinc carbonate, that when it is left exposed to the elements it is rust resistant. These monuments have taken on a "bluish-gray" color as a result of the zinc-carbonate. The term "white bronze" was used only to make the monuments sound expensive.

On March 8, 1939, the Monumental Bronze Company filed for and was granted bankruptcy. They are no longer in business.

W. H. Mullins Company of Salem, Ohio

The W.H. Mullins Company was founded ca. 1894. In addition to the impressive statuary, they also manufactured embossed tin ceilings, architectural pediments and corbels, and an extensive array of lawn and garden ornaments.

The W.H. Mullins Company is still in business in Salem, Ohio.

Monument Building Materials

Monuments were made of four primary materials:

GRANITE

MARBLE

BRONZE

Most Expensive

CAST IRON
(White Bronze)

Least Expensive

Other materials (though used less frequently) for building monuments were:

Sandstone   Brass   Zinc   Copper   Stone

Monument Costs

The cost of a civil war monument was based on several factors:

$ Year the monument was built

$$ Size of the monument

$$$ Materials used to build the monument

The following table demonstrates the fee charged for monuments.

Year	*1870*	**Year**	*1871*
City	*Springfield*	City	*Urbana*
Type	*"Soldier at Parade Rest"*	Type	*"Cavalry Officer"*
Cost	*$10,000*	Cost	*$11,000*
Material	*real bronze*	Material	*sheet copper*
Year	*1893*	**Year**	*1894*
City	*West Union*	City	*Cleveland*
Type	*"Soldier at Parade Rest"*	Type	*"Soldiers & Sailors Monument"*
Cost	*$5,000*	Cost	*$280,000*
Material	*granite*	Material	*granite, bronze, stone*
Year	*1900*	**Year**	*1908*
City	*Salem*	City	*Decatur*
Type	*"Soldier at Parade Rest"*	Type	*"Soldier at Parade Rest"*
Cost	*$1,000*	Cost	*$1,000*
Material	*granite*	Material	*granite*
Year	*1910*	**Year**	*1914*
City	*Ashtabula*	City	*Jefferson*
Type	*"LaGrange Shaft/Eagle"*	Type	*"Soldier at Parade Rest"*
Cost	*$1,330*	Cost	*$700*
Material	*sheet copper*	Material	*white bronze*

Ridgelawn Cemetery
Elyria, Lorain County, Ohio

Types of Monuments

When monument building began in Ohio in the 1860's, the most prominent statues displayed the American Eagle. As monument building continued other characters were displayed, as listed below.

Eagles (3 different poses)

Wings Fully Extended   **Wings Partially Extended**   **Wings Folded**

Soldiers (6 different versions)

Soldier at Parade Rest   **Soldier on Guard**   **Soldier with Flag & Sword**
Color Bearer   **Skirmisher**   **Sentinel**

Obelisk

...... A four-sided monument that tapers to a point

Flag Poles

Artillery Pieces

A Simple Cross

...... Only one in Ohio (New Lexington)

Equestrian Statues

...... Only one in Ohio (Somerset)

Abraham Lincoln

...... Seven throughout the state

Notable Individuals

...... Military & Civilian

Markers and Plaques

...... Marble, stone or bronze

Reedsburg Cemetery - 1887
Reedsburg, Wayne Co., Ohio

Types of Monuments

Structures

...... Gazebos, bandstands, chapels and memorial halls

Confederates

...... Camp Chase - Columbus, Ohio
...... Johnson Island prison site - Marblehead, Ohio
...... Robert E. Lee plaque - Franklin, Ohio
...... Captain William C. Quantrill (Quantrill's Raiders) gravesite - Dover, Ohio

A sample of each monument is displayed on the following pages.

"7th O.V.I. monument"
Woodlawn Cemetery, Cleveland, Ohio

EAGLES

"Partially Extended Wings"
Elyria, Lorain Co., Ohio
copper/concrete

"Fully Extended Wings"
Milan, Erie Co., Ohio
July 4, 1867 - bronze/sandstone

"Folded Wings"
Vienna, Trumbull Co., Ohio
August 31, 1889 - granite

SOLDIERS

"Soldier at Parade Rest"
Waterville, Lucas Co., Ohio

"Soldier with Flag and Sword"
Pittsfield, Lorain Co., Ohio

"Color Bearer"
East Liverpool, Columbiana Co., Ohio

THE OBELISK

North Oregon Cemetery
Oregon, Lucas Co., Ohio

FLAG POLES

Greenlawn Cemetery
Columbus, Franklin Co., Ohio

Veterans Park
Newark, Licking Co., Ohio

ARTILLERY PIECES

Main and First Street
Piqua, Miami Co., Ohio

Ely Park
Elyria, Lorain Co., Ohio

Cedar Grove Cemetery
Peninsula, Summit Co., Ohio

ARTILLERY PIECES

Oakland Cemetery
Warren, Trumbull Co., Ohio

Brimfield Cemetery
Brimfield, Portage Co., Ohio

Sherman House
New Lexington, Perry Co., Ohio

SIMPLE CROSS

Only "Cross Monument" in Ohio

"Veterans Monument Square"
New Lexington, Perry Co., Ohio
July 4, 1876 - granite

EQUESTRIAN STATUE

Only "Equestrian Statue" in Ohio

SHERIDAN

"Village Square"
Somerset, Perry Co., Ohio
November 2, 1905 - bronze/granite

ABRAHAM LINCOLN STATUES

Seven Lincoln statues in Ohio

"Board of Education Building"
Cleveland, Cuyahoga Co., Ohio
February 12, 1932 - bronze/granite

NOTABLE INDIVIDUALS

McPherson Cemetery
General James B. McPherson

Clyde, Sandusky Co., Ohio
June 22, 1881 - $11,000 - bronze/granite

Highest ranking Union Officer killed in batle

NOTABLE INDIVIDUALS

Youngest Major General (age 24) in U.S. Army History

Major General George A. Custer
New Rumley, Harrison Co., Ohio
June 22, 1932 - $15,000 - bronze/granite

MARKERS & PLAQUES

"Standing Rock Cemetery"
Kent, Portage Co., Ohio

"Oakland Cemetery"
Warren, Trumbull Co., Ohio

"Veterans Memorial Park"
Middleport, Meigs Co., Ohio
May 30, 1927

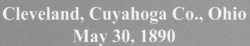

*"President
James A. Garfield
Monument"*
Cleveland, Cuyahoga Co., Ohio
May 30, 1890

CONFEDERATE MARKERS

Camp Chase was established in May 1861, as a training camp for Ohio troops. Later it was expanded and used as a Prisoner of War (POW) Camp for captured Confederates. By 1865, the prison camp held 9,400 prisoners. A total of 2,260 confederates would die while in Camp Chase. They are buried on the grounds of the cemetery. Annotated on a large boulder, located below the arch monument, the following inscription appears:

2,260 Confederate Soldiers of the War
1861 – 1865
Buried in this Enclosure

Camp Chase - Confederate Prison
Columbus, Franklin Co., Ohio

Gravesite of
Captain William C. Quantrill, CSA
Dover, Tuscarawas Co., Ohio

Strange
Different
Unique Monuments

Middleport
Meigs Co., Ohio

Akron, Summit Co., Ohio

Civil War Memorial Chapel
Glendale - Akron Rural Cemetery
Akron, Summit Co., Ohio
Dedicated: May 30, 1876 - Cost: $35,000

Apple Creek, Wayne Co., Ohio

This monument was originally erected near the railroad depot and a dedication ceremony was held (see photographs below) on July 4, 1897. Then, the statue was damaged and a replacement was necessary. The cause of the damage is lost in history. A new statue was dedicated on July 4, 1911 (see photographs on next page). In 1998, a ceremony was held to dedicate the plaque added to the monument. This plaque recognizes Medal of Honor recipient William J. Knight, a native of Apple Creek. Knight was a member of Andrew's Raiders. Knight, the youngest member of the raiding party, served as the train engineer when the Confederate locomotive, The General, was captured in 1862, during the Great Train Robbery.

July 4, 1897 - dedication ceremony

July 4, 1897 - view of monument

Apple Creek, Wayne Co., Ohio

July 4, 1911

Soldier's Monument,
Apple Creek, O.
July 4, 1911.

1914

Apple Creek, Wayne Co., Ohio

William J. Knight - Medal of Honor Recipient

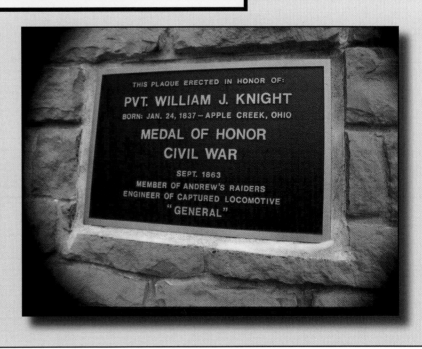

THIS PLAQUE ERECTED IN HONOR OF:
PVT. WILLIAM J. KNIGHT
BORN: JAN. 24, 1837 — APPLE CREEK, OHIO
MEDAL OF HONOR
CIVIL WAR
SEPT. 1863
MEMBER OF ANDREW'S RAIDERS
ENGINEER OF CAPTURED LOCOMOTIVE
"GENERAL"

Apple Creek, Wayne Co., Ohio

"*Railroad Park*"
Apple Creek, Wayne Co., Ohio
Dedicated: July 4, 1897
copper/brick

Bedford, Cuyahoga Co., Ohio

Town Square
Bedford, Cuyahoga Co., Ohio
Dedicated: July 3, 1886
$2,000 - granite

Bellaire, Belmont Co., Ohio

City Park
Bellaire, Belmont Co., Ohio
Dedicated: 1882 - granite

BLUE PAINTED MONUMENTS

Mount View Cemetery
Mt. Vernon, Knox Co., Ohio
bronze/granite

Woodlawn Cemetery
Ohio City, Van Wert Co., Ohio
Dedicated: May 30, 1903
bronze/sandstone

Cambridge, Guernsey Co., Ohio

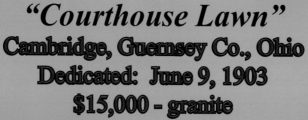

"Courthouse Lawn"
Cambridge, Guernsey Co., Ohio
Dedicated: June 9, 1903
$15,000 - granite

Canton, Stark Co., Ohio

"Westlawn Cemetery"
Canton, Stark Co., Ohio
Dedicated: September 16, 1917
brass/granite

Cleveland, Cuyahoga Co., Ohio

Public Square
Cleveland, Cuyahoga Co., Ohio
Dedicated: July 4, 1894
$230,000 – bronze/granite/stone

"SHORT RANGE"

Depicts artillery at close range

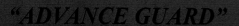

"ADVANCE GUARD"

Depicts two confederate soldiers in hand-to-hand combat with a group of Ohio troops

Cleveland, Cuyahoga Co., Ohio

"MORTAR PRACTICE"

**Depicts the Navy on the Mississippi River
at the Battle of Vicksburg, MS.**

"THE COLOR GUARD"

**Depicts Sgt. Martin Streibler of the 103rd OVI and 8 corporals
who defended their flag at the Battle of Resaca, Georgia
. . . . *All were killed!***

Cuyahoga Falls, Summit Co., Ohio

GAR and "Sultana" Plaque
Oakwood Cemetery
Cuyahoga Falls, Summit Co., Ohio
Dedicated: 1867

Geneva, Ashtabula Co., Ohio

South Eagle Schoolyard
Geneva, Ashtabula Co., Ohio
Dedicated: August 3, 1880
bronze/sandstone

Note: Original location of monument was Main and Broadway. It was moved in 1911.

Greenville, Darke Co., Ohio

Greenville Cemetery
Greenville, Darke Co., Ohio
Dedicated: 1903 - granite

Newark, Licking Co., Ohio

Veterans Park
Newark, Licking Co., Ohio
Dedicated: November 14, 1999

John L. Clem was recognized as being the youngest man to enlist during the civil war (age 9). At the battle of Shiloh, he earned his nickname, "Johnny Shiloh". Following the war, he remained in the Army, having received an Officer's Commission in 1865.

John Clem retired from the Army in 1915, with the rank of Major General.

New Holland, Pickaway Co., Ohio

Town Cemetery
New Holland, Pickaway Co., Ohio
Dedication Date – "unknown"
granite/white bronze

In Holland, Ohio, I located this civil war monument, which <u>was not</u> erected by the town. Instead, it was built to honor the grandchildrens' grandfather. The monument's head was sculptured from a photograph take of the grandfather. The grandchildren paid for the cost of the monument.

New Philadelphia, Tuscarawas Co., Ohio

Courthouse Lawn
New Philadelphia, Tuscarawas Co., Ohio
Dedicated: May 19, 1887 - $5,000 - granite

Peninsula, Summit Co., Ohio

This monument was erected in Peninsula, Ohio, and dedicated on July 4, 1889. The monument was created to honor the veterans from Boston Township, Summit County, Ohio, at a cost $3,000. Originally, it was dedicated and located at the intersection of State Route 303 and Riverview Road in Peninsula, Ohio **(see photograph on next page).** *Being located in the middle of an intersection in 1889, the day of the horse and buggy, did not prove to be a problem. However, when society moved into the automobile age the location of the monument became a problem. In 1932, a motorist ran into the monument, causing the head to fall off. The motorist seized the granite head and sent a ransom note to the authorities, stating that the head would be returned <u>after</u> the monument was moved to a different location. The monument was moved, the head was restored and the monument now resides in Cedar Grove Cemetery, Peninsula, Ohio.*

Peninsula, Summit Co., Ohio

Monument dedication ceremony, July 4, 1889, Peninsula, Ohio

Photograph courtesy of Peninsula Library & Historical Society (Peninsula, Ohio).

Monument's Location:

State Route 303 and Riverview Rds

"Then" and "Now"

Pierpont, Ashtabula Co., Ohio

Th*his monument was originally located at the center of Pierpont, on State Route 7. The monument was moved to the cemetery when traffic became excessive.*
When I visited this monument it was raining quite hard. After I photographed it I retreated to my car, to wait out the storm. As I sat there and observed the statue from afar, I noticed something strange. It appears that the monument's head is not in proportion to the body. Was the original head damage and a replacement made? We may never know.

Evergreen Cemetery
Pierpont, Ashtabula Co., Ohio

Sandusky, Erie Co., Ohio

"Welcome Home"
Old Soldier's Home
Sandusky, Erie Co., Ohio
Dedicated: September 17, 1988 - bronze

Uhrichsville, Tuscarawas Co., Ohio

Union Cemetery
Uhrichsville, Tuscarawas Co., Ohio
Dedicated: May 30, 1891 – sandstone

Washington C.H., Fayette Co., Ohio

n 2004, I visited the cemetery in Washington C.H., Ohio, to locate and photograph their civil war monument. After a considerable period of time scouring the grounds, with no success, I visited the cemetery's records office. I spoke with the manager and explained why I was visiting his cemetery. At that point he turned and pointed. There, standing in the corner, was the civil war monument.

The cast iron ("white bronze") statue had suffered over the years due to weather conditions, and perhaps, cemetery vandalism. I was told that the statue had been moved into the office to protect it from further damage until a decision could be made regarding it's ultimate fate (i.e., repair, replacement or destruction).

Local Cemetery
Washington C.H., Fayette Co., Ohio
cast iron (white bronze)

Wauseon, Fulton Co., Ohio

"Local Park"
Wauseon, Fulton Co., Ohio
Base Erected: 1867
bronze/sandstone

Monument was not completed &
dedicated until 1918

"Courthouse Lawn"
Wauseon, Fulton Co., Ohio
Dedicated: July 4, 1921
$4,000 - zinc

Total Monuments & Locations

I have identified and photographed 270 civil war monuments throughout the state of Ohio. Have I located them all? Probably not. If I missed the one in your town, please let me know. I assure you it was not due to a lack of effort on my part. More than six years of research went into this book.

To assist those individuals who would like to visit the monument discussed in this book, as well as the other monuments throughout Ohio, I provide the following tables. Each one is sorted based on an Ohio Region (see map below). Within the Region Table, a further sort is done based on the County and City.

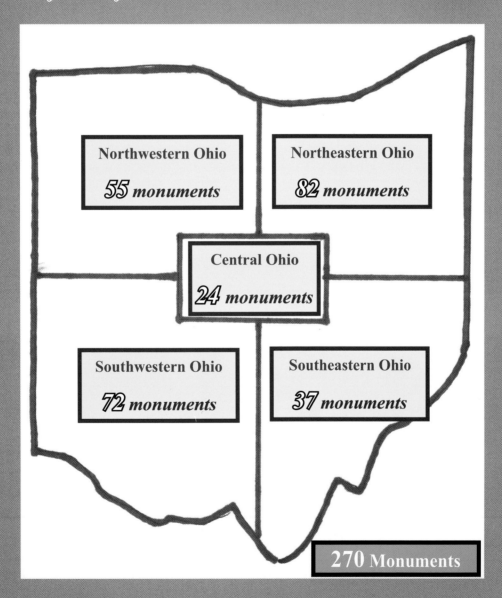

Northwestern Ohio

55 monuments

Northeastern Ohio

82 monuments

Central Ohio

24 monuments

Southwestern Ohio

72 monuments

Southeastern Ohio

37 monuments

270 Monuments

NORTHWEST OHIO

COUNTY	CITY	LOCATION	TYPE OF MONUMENT
Allen	Lafayette	High Street	Soldier at parade rest
	Lima	Woodlawn Cemetery	Soldier monument
	Spencerville	Township Cemetery	Obelisk with eagle on top
Auglaize	St. Mary's	Elm Grove Cemetery	Soldier at parade rest
	Wapakoneta	Greenlawn Cemetery	Soldier at parade rest
Crawford	Oceola	Stanley's Farm - N. Rt. 30	Granite boulder w/inscription
Defiance	Defiance	Riverside Cemetery	Soldier at parade rest
	Hicksville	Forest Home Cemetery	Soldier at parade rest
	Sherwood	Sherwood Cemetery	Soldier at parade rest
Fulton	Wauseon	Courthouse Lawn	Soldier at parade rest
	Wauseon	Park on State Route 2	Officer w/saber on pedestal
Hancock	Findlay	Maple Grove Cemetery	Soldier at parade rest
	Fostoria	Fountain Cemetery	Soldier at parade rest
	McComb	McComb Union Cemetery	Soldier at parade rest
Hardin	Ada	Village Park	Cannon on top of base
	Kenton	Grove Cemetery	Grave J. Parrott/MOH Andrews Raider
	Kenton	Grove Cemetery	Soldier at parade rest
Henry	McClure	State Route 6	Cannon on stone blocks
Lucas	Maumee	102 E. Broadway	Soldier at parade rest
	Monclova Twp.	Monclova Cemetery	Obelisk w/eagle
	Oregon	Willow Cemetery	Soldier at parade rest
	Oregon	North Oregon Cemetery	Obelisk
	Toledo	Galena at Summit Rd.	Gen. Steedman mon.
	Toledo	325 Michigan Street	Eternal flame
	Toledo	Woodlawn Cemetery	Col. H. Neubert grave
	Toledo	Woodlawn Cemetery	Gen Steedman grave
	Toledo	Forest Cemetery	Grave G. Forsyth, POW died 1864
	Toledo	Woodlawn Cemetery	Obelisk
	Toledo	Civic Center Plaza	Civil War urn
	Toledo	Forest Cemetery	Mon. to CW widows
	Toledo	Forest Cemetery	Grave M. Wood, MOH/Andrews Raider
	Toledo	Wakeman Cemetery	Soldier at parade rest
	Whitehouse	Town Square	Soldier at parade rest
Marion	Marion	620 Delaware	Soldier/Sailor Memorial
Mercer	Mendon	Market and Main St.	Soldier at parade rest
Morrow	Cardington	Glendale Cemetery	Soldier at parade rest
Ottawa	Johnson's Island	Confederate Cemetery	"Southern Soldier" monument
Putnam	Columbus Grove	Plum and Sycamore St.	Soldier at parade rest

N O R T H W E S T   O H I O

COUNTY	CITY	LOCATION	TYPE OF MONUMENT
Sandusky	Bellevue	Bellevue Cemetery	Grave Col. C. B.Gambee - 55th OVI
	Clyde	Route 20 and 101	Gen J. B. McPherson monument
	Fremont	423 Crogham Street	Soldier at parade rest
Seneca	Tiffin	Adams & N. Monroe	"Standard Bearer" monument
	Tiffin	Courthouse Lawn	Gen William H. Gibson monument
VanWert	Delphos	302 West Second St.	Soldier at parade rest
	Ohio City	Woodlawn Cemetery	Soldier at parade rest
	Van Wert	Woodland Cemetery	Soldier at parade rest
	Van Wert	Courthouse Lawn	Cannon on base
Williams	Edgerton	Rt 6 & Rt 49 park	Soldier at parade rest
Wood	Bowling Green	Union Hill Cemetery	Grave J. A. Wilson/MOH (Andrews Raider)
	Perrysburg	Louisiana & Front St.	Standard bearer monument
	Wayne	Church & Main St.	Soldier at parade rest
	Weston	Weston Cemetery	Soldier at parade rest
Wyandot	Nevada	Nevada Cemetery	Granite monument
	Sycamore	Old Sycamore Cemetery	GAR monument
	Upper Sandusky	Courthouse	Bronze Marker/GAR

NORTHEAST OHIO

COUNTY	CITY	LOCATION	TYPE OF MONUMENT
Ashland	Ashland	Courthouse Lawn	Soldier at parade rest
Ashtabula	Ashtabula	44th and Main St.	Obelisk w/eagle
	Austinburg	West of Rt 45 & 307	Soldier at parade rest
	Conneaut	Liberty St. Cemetery	Soldier at parade rest
	Geneva	119 S. Eagle St.	Soldiers & Sailors monument
	Jefferson	Courthouse Lawn	Soldier at parade rest
	Pierpont	Evergreen Cemetery	Soldier at parade rest
	Windsor	Noble Road Cemetery	Soldier at parade rest
Columbiana	East Liverpool	Riverview Cemetery	Soldier at parade rest
	Salem	Hope Cemetery	E.C. Memorial obelisk
	Salem	Grandview Cemetery	"Color Bearer" statue
	Salem	Hope Cemetery	Soldier at parade rest #1
	Salem	Hope Cemetery	Soldier at parade rest #2
	West Point	State Rt 518	Granite boulder (Morgan)
Coshocton	New Castle	Town Center	Obelisk
Cuyahoga	Bedford	Public Square	Soldier at parade rest
	Cleveland	Public Square	Soldiers & Sailors Mon.
	Cleveland	Lakeview Cemetery	Gen. Garfield monument
	Cleveland	East 6th Street	A. Lincoln statue
	Cleveland	Lakeview Cemetery	Grave Major. M. Leggett
	Cleveland	Woodlawn Cemetery	7th OVI monument
	Cleveland	Woodlawn Cemetery	23rd OVI monument
Erie	Milan	Park Square	Tall Obelisk w/eagle
	Sandusky	Ohio Veterans Home	"Coming Home" monument
	Sandusky	Ohio Vets Home Cemetery	Tall Obelisk
	Sandusky	Ohio Vets Home Cemetery	Gazebo
Geauga	Montville	Montville Cemetery	five-tier granite monument
Huron	New London	Monument Park	Soldier at parade rest
Lake	Madison	Town Square	Soldier at parade rest
	Painesville	Veterans Memorial Park	Soldier at parade rest
	Willoughby	Town Square	Soldier at parade rest
Lorain	Elyria	Ridgelawn Cemetery	"Skirmisher" monument
	Elyria	Ridgelawn Cemetery	Eagle with outspread wings
	Elyria	Ely Park	"Standard Bearer" atop tall column
	Grafton	Butternut Ridge Cemetery	Soldier at parade rest
	Huntington	Routes 58 and 162	Eagle atop tall obelisk
	Kipton	Sixth and State Streets	Soldier at parade rest
	LaGrange	Routes 301 and 303	"Standard Bearer" atop tall column
	Oberlin	S. Main and W. Vine	Memorial Wall
	Oberlin	S. Professor Street	Gen Giles Shurtleff statue
	Oberlin	E. Vine Street	Shaft honoring 3 blacks with John Brown

NORTHEAST OHIO

COUNTY	CITY	LOCATION	TYPE OF MONUMENT
Lorain	Oberlin	Professor & W. College	Underground Railroad monument
	Oberlin	E. Vine Street	Monument to Wellington/Oberlin Rescue
	Pittsfield	Routes 58 & 303	Soldier at parade rest
Mahoning	Youngstown	Center Square	Soldier at parade rest
Medina	Chatham	Routes 83 & 162	Obelisk with eagle on top
	Medina	Spring Grove Cemetery	Soldier at parade rest
	Wadsworth	Woodlawn Cemetery	Soldier with flag & Sword
Portage	Kent	Standing Rock Cemetery.	Grave N. H. Hall MOH winner
	Nelson	Route 305	Four-tiered pedestal - Eagle on top
	Ravenna	Maple Grove Cemetery	Gravesite for two slaves in Ravenna
Richland	Mansfield	Central Park	Soldier at parade rest
	Mansfield	South Park	Soldier at parade rest
	Mansfield	South Park	Historic Marker - "Sultana" disaster
Richmond	Mansfield	Central Park	Abraham Lincoln bronze plaque
Stark	Alliance	Alliance Public Square	Abraham Lincoln statue
	Canton	Westlawn Cemetery	Soldier at parade rest
	East Sparta	Cemetery	Soldier at parade rest
	Massillon	Town Center	Cannon with plaques
	Navarre	Union Lawn Cemetery	Soldiers' monument
	Wilmot	Greenlawn Cemetery	Soldier at parade rest
Summit	Akron	Glendale Cemetery	Civil War chapel
	Cuyahoga Falls	Oakwood Cemetery	Civil War Vets & "Sultana" obelisk
	Peninsula	Cedar Grove Cemetery	Soldier at parade rest
	Twinsburg	Town Square	Pillar topped with an eagle
Trumbull	Bristolville	State Routes 45 and 88	Funeral Urn on a square base
	Mesopotamia	State Routes 534 and 87	Eagle atop a tall shaft
	Niles	West Park Avenue	Eagle atop a square pillar
	Southington	Routes 305 and 534	Soldier at parade rest/tall column
	Vienna	Rt 193 & Warren/Sharon	Eagle atop a tall shaft
	Warren	Oakwood Cemetery	GAR granite slab memorial
	Warren	Main and High Streets	Monument with three soldiers
Tuscarawas	Dover	Fourth Street Cemetery	Gravesite W.C. Quantrill (conf. Raider)
	Dover	Maple Grove Cemetery	Soldier at parade rest
	New Philadelphia	Courthouse Lawn	Soldier at parade rest
	Ragersville	Ragersville Cemetery	Eagle atop an obelisk
	Uhrichsville	Union Cemetery	Soldiers' monument
Wayne	Apple Creek	Railroad Park	Soldier at parade rest
	Reedsburg	Reedsburg Cemetery	Obelisk topped with 13 cannon balls
	Wooster	Public Square	Soldier at parade rest
	Wooster	Andrew's Library	Abraham Lincoln statue
	Wooster	Wooster Cemetery	Soldier at parade rest

"These Are My Jewels"

Capital Square, Columbus, Franklin Co., Ohio

Monument depicting bronze statues of seven famous Ohioans:
U. S. Grant, William T. Sherman, James Garfield, Rutherford B. Hayes, Edwin Stanton, Salmon P. Chase and Philip Sheridan

CENTRAL OHIO

COUNTY	CITY	LOCATION	TYPE OF MONUMENT
Clark	Springfield	Ferncliff Cemetery	Soldier at parade rest
Delaware	Delaware	Courthouse Lawn	Soldier at parade rest
	Sunbury	Rosecrans Road	Plaque/bolder - Gen Rosecrans birthplace
Fairfield	Canal Winchester	N. High & W. Oaks	Monument to honor Private. Alfred Cannon
	Lancaster	East Main Street	Birthplace Gen. William T. Sherman
Franklin	Columbus	Capital Rotunda	Lincoln & Vicksburg memorial
	Columbus	Sullivant Avenue	Site of Camp Chase and rebel prison
	Columbus	Greenlawn Cemetery	Soldier at parade rest
	Columbus	Greenlawn Cemetery	Veterans flag pole memorial
	Columbus	Capital Square	Peace monument/bronze female figure
	Columbus	Capital Square	Civil War Leaders bronze monument
	Columbus	Greenlawn Cemetery	Gravesite J.O.Smith-MOH-Andrews Raider
	Columbus	Capital Plaza	Sundial
	Westerville	160 W. Main Street	Home of Ben Hanby (Darling Nellie Gray)
	Westerville	Towers-Otterbein College	Monument to 100 men associated w/Otterbein
Knox	Mt. Vernon	Mont View Cemetery	Soldier at parade rest
	Mt. Vernon	Monument Square	Soldier at parade rest on tall column
	Mt. Vernon	Route 3 City Cemetery	Gravesite of D.D. Emmett (author of "Dixie")
Licking	Newark	Veterans Park 6th & Main	Johnny Clem monument
	Newark	Veterans Park 6th & Main	Veterans flag pole memorial
Madison	London	Oak Hill Cemetery	Soldier at parade rest
Union	Milford Center	Milford Center Cemetery	Eagle with spread wings atop a tall shaft
	New California	US 42 & Industrial Pkwy	Soldier at parade rest

SOUTHWEST OHIO

COUNTY	CITY	LOCATION	TYPE OF MONUMENT
Adams	West Union	Town Square	Soldier at parade rest
Brown	Decatur	Decatur Park	Soldier at parade rest
	East Ripley	Maplewood Cemetery	Soldier at parade rest
	Georgetown	Water Street	U.S. Grant's school house
	Georgetown	Route 125	U.S. Grant's birthplace
	Red Oak	Presbyterian Graveyard	Gravesite of Rose W. Riles ("Aunt Jemima")
	Ripley	Front and Mulberry	Wood plaque on tree
	Ripley	Public Library	Cannon and memorial plaque to Battery "F"
	Ripley	Liberty Hill	Home of Rev. John Rankin (underground RR)
	Ripley	Front and Main	Liberty monument for Rev. John Rankin
	Ripley	Front Street	Home of John Parker (underground RR)
	Ripley	Front Street	Granite slab for Ripley underground RR role
	Sardinia	Old Sardinia Cemetery	Gravesite Rev. John Mahan (anti-slave)
Butler	Hamilton	High & Monument Streets	Butler Co. Soldiers & Sailors monument
	Hamilton	Monument Street	Plaque next to Butler Co. monument
	Middletown	Woodside Cemetery	Soldier holding gun, atop stone base
Champaign	Mechanicsburg	Maple Grove Cemetery	Soldier at parade rest
	Urbana	Monument Square	Cavalry Officer - head bowed
Clermont	Laurel	Laurel Methodist Church	Stained Glass Window (home of. US Grant)
	Pt. Pleasant	U.S. 52	Birthplace of U.S. Grant
	Pt. Pleasant	U.S. 52	Grant Memorial Bridge
	Stone Lick Twp.	State Route 50	Cannon on brick base
	Williamsburg	Township Cemetery	Soldier at parade rest
Darke	Greenville	Greenville Cemetery	Soldier at parade rest
Fayette	Washington C.H.	Washington Cemetery	Soldier at parade rest(kept in office-damaged)
Green	Wilberforce	Massies Creek Cemetery	Grave of Martin Delany (recruiter 54th Mass)
	Yellow Springs	Antioch Hall College	Plaque honor 33 school students killed in war
Hamilton	Blue Ash	Town Square	Bicentennial Veterans Memorial
	Blue Ash	Town Square	Millennium American Heritage Bell Tower
	Cincinnati	Rockdale & Forest Rds.	Lincoln/Liberty monument
	Cincinnati	Lytle Park	Abraham Lincoln statue
	Cincinnati	Piatt Park	President Garfield monument
	Cincinnati	1225 Elm Street	Hamilton County Memorial Bridge
	Cincinnati	Washington Park	Bust of Brig. General Hecker - US Army
	Cincinnati	Washington Park	Colonel Robert McCook monument
	Cincinnati	Spring Grove Cemetery	"The Sentinel" monument
	Cincinnati	Spring Grove Cemetery	Monument for 5th OVI
	Cincinnati	Spring Grove Cemetery	Grave of General William H. Lytle
	Cincinnati	Spring Grove Cemetery	Monument for "Fighting McCooks"
	Cincinnati	Spring Grove Cemetery	Cannon dedicated to "Unknown Dead"
	Cincinnati	Alms Park	Stephen Foster statue

S O U T H W E S T   O H I O

COUNTY	CITY	LOCATION	TYPE OF MONUMENT
Hamilton	*Cincinnati*	*Eden Park*	*GAR Flagstaff*
	Indian Hill	*St. Rt. 126 & Kugler Mill*	*Plaque on boulder for Camp Dennison*
Highland	*Greenfield*	*Greenfield Cemetery*	*Soldier at parade rest*
	Hillsboro	*Courthouse Lawn*	*Soldier on top/Drummer boy at base of mon.*
	Hillsboro	*Courthouse Lawn*	*Monument to unknown dead*
	Lynchburg	*High & Sycamore Cem.*	*Obelisk monument*
Logan	*Bellefontaine*	*Bellefontaine Cemetery*	*Tall square shaped monument*
Miami	*Piqua*	*Hardin Road*	*Bronze marker for 94th & 110th OVI*
	Piqua	*Jackson Cemetery*	*Plaque on boulder for Randolph slaves*
	Piqua	*Forest Hill Cemetery*	*Tall obelisk with carved eagle*
	Piqua	*East Main & First Streets*	*Replica cannon on granite base*
	Pleasant Hills	*Town Center*	*Soldier at parade rest*
	Troy	*Riverside Cemetery*	*Soldier at parade rest*
Montgomery	*Dayton*	*Main St/North Gateway*	*Soldier at parade rest*
	Dayton	*4100 West Third St.*	*Soldier at parade rest*
	Dayton	*4100 West Third St.*	*Soldier at parade rest with 4 figures*
	Dayton	*Woodland Arboretum*	*Obelisk*
	Dayton	*Woodland Cemetery*	*Grave for Clement Vallandigham*
Pickaway	*Circleville*	*905 North Court Street*	*Soldier at parade rest*
	New Holland	*Town Cemetery*	*Soldier at parade rest (private monument)*
Preble	*Eaton*	*Route 122*	*Soldier at parade rest*
	Eaton	*Route 122*	*"Skirmisher"*
Ross	*Chillicothe*	*Yoctangee Park*	*Soldier at parade rest*
	Chillicothe	*Grandview Cemetery*	*Soldier at parade rest*
	Chillicothe	*Grandview Cemetery*	*Grave monument for Gen. Joshua W. Sill*
Scioto	*Portsmouth*	*9th & Chilicothe Streets*	*"Standard Bearer"*
	Portsmouth	*Greenlawn Cemetery*	*Soldiers Circle Chapel*
	Portsmouth	*Greenlawn Cemetery*	*Soldier at parade rest*
Shelby	*Sidney*	*Court & Ohio Streets*	*"Soldier in Blue" monument*
	Sidney	*Ohio & Main Streets*	*Marker to Schultz's Battery*
Warren	*Franklin*	*Hamilton & Middletown*	*Two cannons and flag pole*
	Franklin	*Hamilton & Middletown*	*Plaque on boulder to Robert E. Lee*

Willow Cemetery
Oregon, Lucas County, Ohio

S O U T H E A S T   O H I O

COUNTY	CITY	LOCATION	TYPE OF MONUMENT
Athens	Athens	Ohio University	Bronze sailor atop a tall monument
	Athens	West Elementary School	Camp Wood marker on boulder
	Doanville	Greenlawn Cemetery	Cannon on cement slab
Belmont	Bellaire	Belmont St. & 34th	Soldier at parade rest
	Bridgeport	Weeks Cemetery	War Memorial and cannon
Carroll	Carrollton	Public Square	McCook House
Gallia	Gallipolis	City Park	Bandstand
Guernsey	Cambridge	Courthouse Lawn	Soldier at parade rest
	Cambridge	Old Cambridge Cemetery	Obelisk monument for unknown dead
Harrison	Cadiz	Courthouse Lawn	John A. Bingham monument
	Cadiz	Courthouse Lawn	Historic marker for Bishop Matthew Simpson
	New Rumley	County Road 646	General George A. Custer monument
Hocking	Logan	Town Square	Soldier at parade rest
Holmes	Millersburg	Town Square	Soldier at parade rest
Jackson	Jackson	Main & Broadway Street	Bronze plaque for Civil War soldiers
	Wellston	Town Square	Soldier at parade rest (base only)
	Wellston	Town Square	Iron Cannon
Jefferson	Bravo	County Roads 53 & 54	Cannon on stone shaft
	Steubenville	3rd & Market Streets	Edwin M Stanton monument
	Steubenville	Union Cemetery	Monument to CW Unknown Dead
	Steubenville	Union Cemetery	Plaque on granite slab
	Steubenville	Union Cemetery	Eagle atop a tall column
Lawrence	Ironton	Woodlawn Cemetery	Four Parrott Rifles
Meigs	Middleport	Mill & South 5th Avenue	Gazebo
	Pomeroy	West Second & Court St.	"Soldier on Guard"
	Portland	State Route 124	Major Daniel McCook monument
	Portland	Buffington Island Park	Union/Confederate historic markers
	Portland	State Route 124	Monument to capture John Hunt Morgan
Monroe	Antioch	State Route 800	Soldier at parade rest
Morgan	Eagleport	Rt 60, South of Rokeby	Granite monument to Morgan's Raid
	McConnelsville	Town Square	Union Soldier with Rifle
Muskingum	Zanesville	Hamlin & Greenwood	Soldier at parade rest
Perry	New Lexington	S. Main St & Route 13	Cross monument to 30th OVI - only 1 in Ohio
	Somerset	Village Square	Gen Philip Sheridan mon (only one in state)
Vinton	McArthur	Courthouse Lawn	Soldier at parade rest
Washington	Marietta	Front & Putnam Streets	Soldier at parade rest w/four Parrott guns
	Newport	Cemetery	Names of Newport Twp citizens (on base)

Union Cemetery - 1894
McComb, Hancock Co., Ohio

Bibliography

- Kachur, Thomas J.   ***"Historical Collections of Bristol Township, Bristolville, Ohio",*** 1989, Bristolville Public Library
- Butler County   ***"Soldiers, Sailors & Pioneers Monument"*** brochure (undated)

- ***"Cuyahoga Valley"*** **Cuyahoga Valley Historical Museum and Cuyahoga Valley National Park Association** ©2004
- ***"Timeline"*** magazine **Ohio Historical Society** publication ©2003, regarding the Soldiers and Sailors Monument, Public Square, Cleveland, Ohio
- ***"A Tribute to Civil War Veterans"***
    Cleveland Plain Dealer newspaper article, Tuesday, November 11, 2003
- ***"To Those Who Brave Horrors of War"***
    Cleveland Plain Dealer newspaper, Tuesday, November 11, 2003
- ***Internet References:***
    1   Ohio in the Civil War - *www.ohiocivilwar.com*
    2   W.H. Mullins Co. of Salem, Ohio - *www.antiques.com & www.dragonflycanoe.com*
    3   Cincinnati Historical Society - *www.chs.org*
    4   Connecticut Historical Society - *www.chs.org*
    5   Butler County, Butler, Ohio - *www.butlercounty.org*
    6   Civil War Monuments of Maryland - *www.sos.state.m.us*
    7   Civil War Monuments of New York State - *www.morrisville.cu*
    8   Oberlin Walking Tours of Civil War Monuments - *www.oberlin.edu*
    9   Testament to Union - *www.cw.book.news.com*
    10   Ohio Outdoor Sculpture Inventory - *www.sculptercenter.org*
    11   Smithsonian Institution Research - *www.siris.si.edu*

Photograph Sources

The photograph, ***Boston Township Soldiers Monument"*** depicting the dedication ceremony held on July 4, 1889, in Peninsula, Ohio, is from the collection of the Peninsula Public Library and Historical Society (Peninsula, Ohio).

The black and white photographs of the Apple Creek civil war monuments are from the collection of Joseph Lackman, local historian, Apple Creek, Ohio.

Permissions

The photograph, ***"Boston Township Soldiers Monument",*** is used with the permission of Randy Bergdorf, Peninsula Public Library and Cuyahoga Valley Historical Museum.

The black and white photographs of the Apple Creek monuments are used with the permission of Joseph Lackman, of Apple Creek, Ohio.

The information contained in the internet web site, www.chs.org is used with the permission of Ms. Anne Kling, Archives Manager, Cincinnati Historical Society Library, per telephone call with the author on December 21, 2005.

Ohio University - 1893
Athens, Athens Co., Ohio

About the Author

Harold George retired from the Department of Defense, U.S. Navy, in 1995, after a 29-year career. In 1982, while still working the government, George began presenting lecture programs for the public. Each program pertained to a different historical event.

In 1992, George began his career as a civil war re-enactor, assigned to the 9th Ohio IB of Light Artillery. Over the last fourteen years George continued as re-enactor, rising to his current rank of 1st Lieutenant and serves as the commanding officer of the artillery unit.

In 2003, George published his civil war/genealogical book, "Men of the 9th Ohio". More than eight-years of research were necessary for the book to be completed.

To date, George has developed six-different video/lecture programs, which he performs for numerous organizations throughout the year. His current book, Civil War Monuments of Ohio, required six-years of research to complete.

George lives at home with his lovely wife, Camilla, in Lakewood, Ohio. When he is not performing programs for the public, re-enacting, or doing research on a future project, he enjoys fishing, photography, and travel.

Hope Cemetery - 1900
Salem, Columbiana Co., Ohio

Woodlawn Cemetery
Wadsworth, Medina Co., Ohio

Talks and Other Publications Available

Author's Books

"Chasing Ghosts! - - In Search of Relatives Who Fought in the War Between the States: 1865-65"

"Men of the 9th Ohio - An Illustrated History of the 9th Ohio Independent Battery of Light Artillery"

"Statues in Time - - Civil War Monuments of Ohio"

Author's Publications

"Arlington National Cemetery - - A Quick Reference Guide to Arlington National Cemetery"
"Custer's Last Stand - - A Quick Reference Guide to the Battle of the Little Bighorn"

Video Lecture Programs

"Men of the 9th Ohio - - One Man's Hunt for Civil War Gravesites!"
"Life of a Civil War Soldier : 1861-65"
*"Custer's Last Stand" The Myth * The Legend * The Truth!"*
"Arlington National Cemetery - - The Home of America's Heroes"
"Statues in Time - - Civil War Monuments of Ohio"
"The Aftermath at Gettysburg"

* * *

All programs are professionally performed and ideal for libraries, historical societies, Civil War roundtables, veterans organizations, high school students and church groups. The author has presented his programs since 1982.

To inquire about any of the above publications or to arrange for a video program, please contact the author at one of the following:

Address: **Harold A. George**
            14513 Bayes Avenue
            Lakewood, Ohio 44107

Telephone: **216-319-4575**

Email: **ninthohio@core.com**